The Bible FUN BOOK NO. 1

LARRY STEVE CRAIN

WestBow Press books may be ordered through booksellers or by contacting:

WestBow Press
A Division of Thomas Nelson
1663 Liberty Drive
Bloomington, IN 47403
www.westbowpress.com
1 (866) 928-1240

Because of the dynamic nature of the Internet, any web addresses or links contained in this book may have changed
since publication and may no longer be valid. The views expressed in this work are solely those of the author and do
not necessarily reflect the views of the publisher, and the publisher hereby disclaims any responsibility for them.

Purchase of this book entitles you to copy pages from this book and distribute those
copies to your children, Sunday school class members, and elsewhere.

ISBN: 978-1-4908-1563-3 (sc)
ISBN: 978-1-4908-1564-0 (e)

Library of Congress Control Number: 2013921023

Printed in the United States of America.

WestBow Press rev. date: 12/03/2013

WestBow
PRESS
A DIVISION OF THOMAS NELSON

How It All Began

GOD MADE THE ⭐ AND THE EARTH. THEN GOD MADE 🌳 AND 🍎 AND 🥕 AND MUCH MORE. THEN HE MADE THE ☀ FOR DAY AND THE 🌙 FOR NIGHT. NEXT GOD MADE 🐟 AND 🕊 AND 🐕 AND 🦋 AND MANY MORE. AND GOD SAW THAT IT WAS ALL VERY GOOD. THEN GOD MADE A 🚶 CALLED "ADAM" AND A 🧍 CALLED "EVE." THAT IS HOW IT ALL BEGAN.

God Made Many Animals. Can You Finish Drawing this Dog?

3

What Does This Code Say?

$\underline{\quad}$ $\underline{\quad}$ $\underline{\quad}$ $\underline{\quad}$ $\underline{\quad}$ $\underline{\quad}$ $\underline{\quad}$ $\underline{\quad}$ $\underline{\quad}$ $\underline{\quad}$.
7 15 4   12 15 22 5 19   13 5

A	B	C	D	E	F	G	H	I	J
1	2	3	4	5	6	7	8	9	10

K	L	M	N	O	P	Q	R	S
11	12	13	14	15	16	17	18	19

T	U	V	W	X	Y	Z
20	21	22	23	24	25	26

The wise men followed a star to find Jesus Christ.

Baby Jesus Was Laid in a Manger.

Help the Wise Men Find the Christ Child's House!

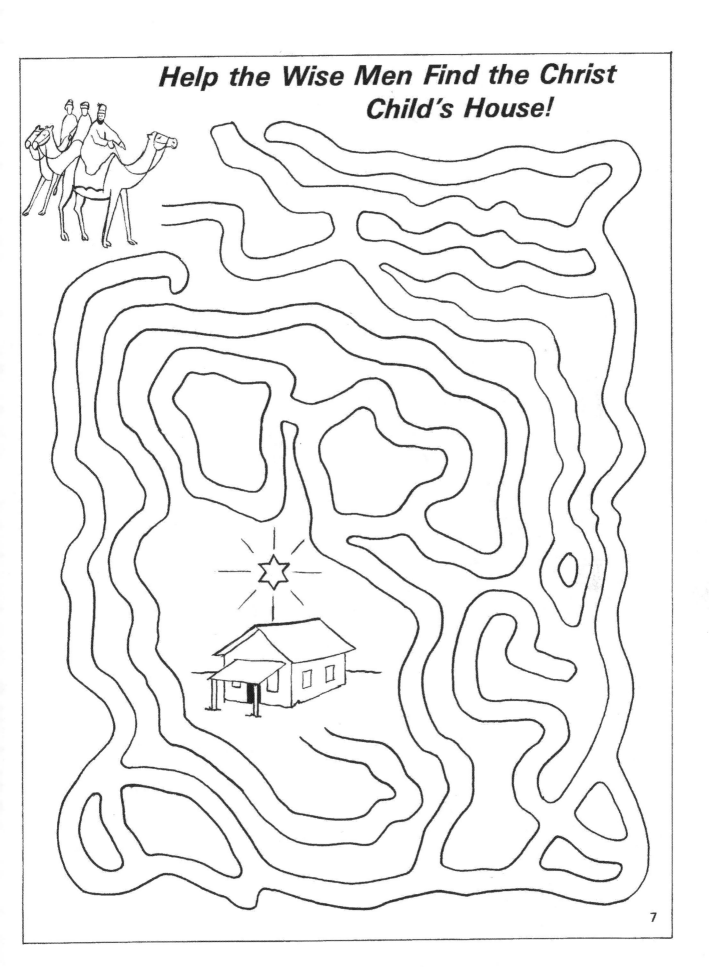

Jesus Grew Up in His Earthly Father's Carpenter Shop.

CONNECT THE DOTS!

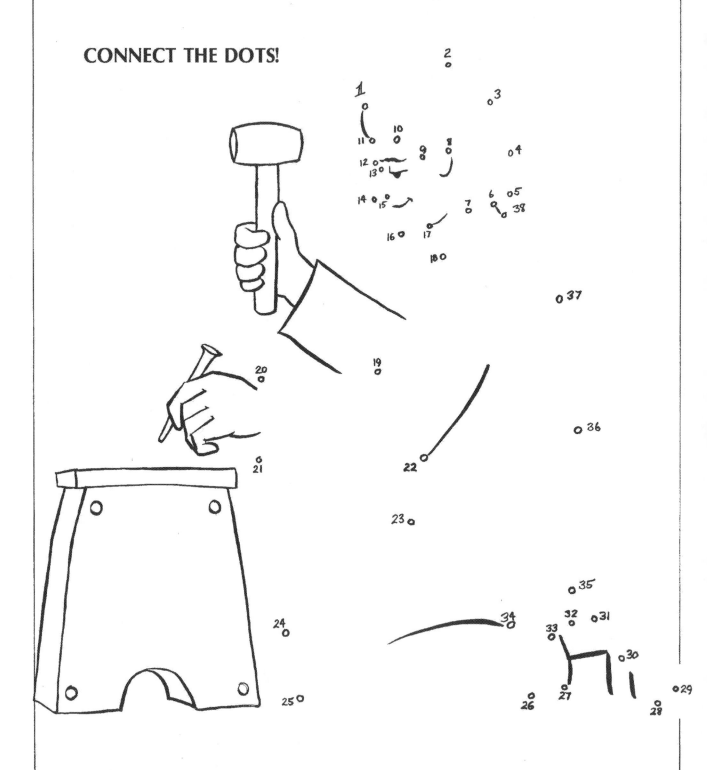

John Baptized Jesus in the Jordan River.

The Holy Spirit Came to Jesus in the Form of a Dove.

What Did Jesus Tell the People?

ANSWER: THE WAY

Help the Shepherd Find the Lost Sheep.

START

BA-BA

12

Jesus fed 5,000 people with which foods?

① ② ③

Connect the dots to see Jesus talking to the woman at the well.

JOHN 4:4-42

Jesus said, "Come to me."

MATT. 11:28

Sue Is Lost. Help Her
Get to Jesus.

16

What Did Jesus Ride into Jerusalem?

Connect the Dots!

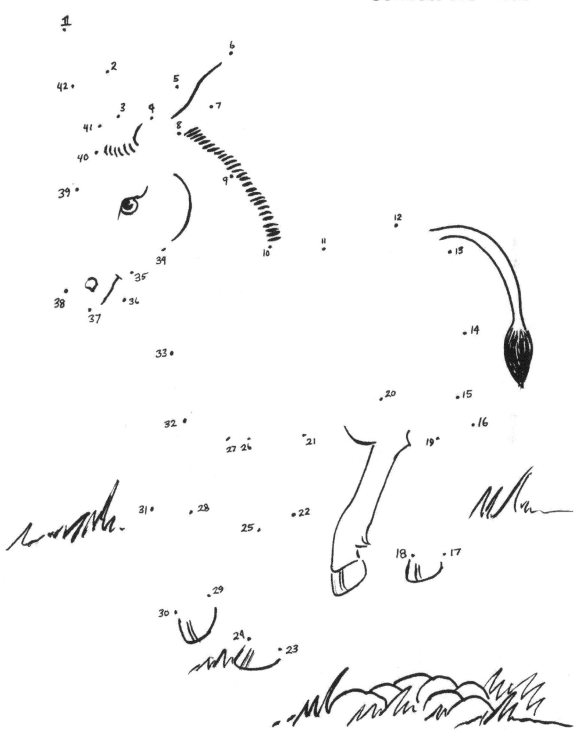

Jesus Healed Many Sick People.

We Should Talk to God the Father in Prayer.

— I TIMOTHY 2:8

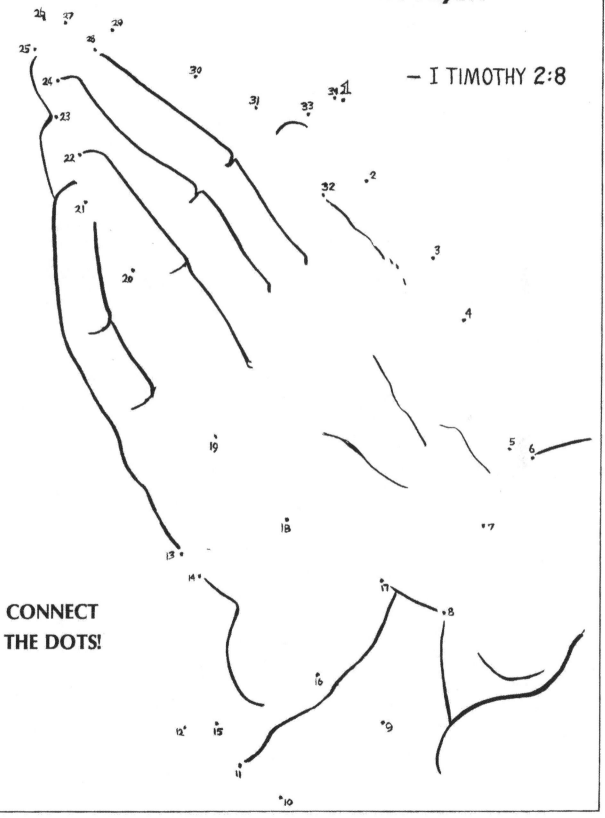

CONNECT THE DOTS!

From Which Creature's Mouth Did Peter Get Money to Pay His Taxes?

SEE: MATTHEW 17:27

20

Here's a Message for You!

THE 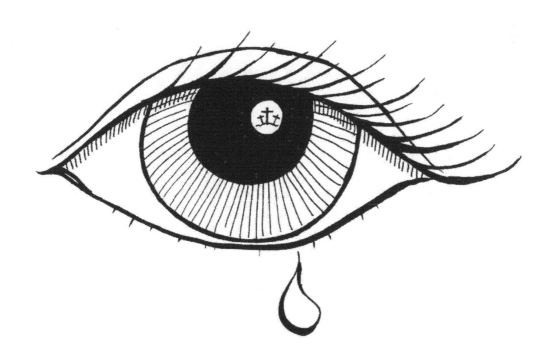 SAYS THAT JESUS DIED ON THE ✝ FOR ME. 👁 TRY TO 🐝 AS GOOD AS 👁 🥫🌾 BUT JESUS HAS 2 MAKE ME GOOD ENOUGH. IF 👁 ASK JESUS 2 COME N-2 MY ♡ THEN 👁 WILL 🐝 ☺. 👁 CAN REALLY LIVE!

What Does This Code Say?

7	15	4		1	14	19	23	5	18	19

16	18	1	25	5	18		20	15	4	1	25

A	B	C	D	E	F	G	H	I	J
1	2	3	4	5	6	7	8	9	10

K	L	M	N	O	P	Q	R	S
11	12	13	14	15	16	17	18	19

T	U	V	W	X	Y	Z
20	21	22	23	24	25	26

Zaccheus Climbed a Tree to See Jesus. 23

Jesus Said, "Blessed Are the Peacemakers."

Some People Did Not Like Jesus.
Can You Find Six Swords in This Picture?

**Jesus Said to Eat the Lord's Supper
and Remember Him.**

Judas Betrayed Jesus with a Kiss.

Jesus Died for Our Sins.

But He Rose from the Dead.

Tim Wants to Go to Heaven.
Help Him Get There by Way of the Cross.

Jesus Wants to Save You and Fill You with His Holy Spirit.

**Jesus Loves You. Draw Yourself
Standing Beside Jesus.**

God says we should respect the policemen and our laws. Help this officer find this little girl's house.

33

Rom. 13:1-5

All have sinned and come short of the glory of God. Rom. 3:23

BECAUSE ALL HAVE SINNED, JESUS HAD TO DIE TO PAY FOR OUR SINS.

B

Believe on the Lord Jesus Christ and you will be saved. Acts 16:31

Draw a face on the soldier.

Children, obey your parents in the Lord, for this is right. Eph. 6:1

CONNECT THE DOTS

D

Depart from evil and do good.
Psa. 34:14

Help Sam go to Jesus.

37

Even a child is known by his doings.
Prov. 20:11

38

CONNECT THE DOTS

Fear not, for I am with you.
Gen. 26:24

Draw hands on the clock.

39

God is love. 1 John 4:8

CONNECT THE DOTS

H

Honor your father and your mother.
Ex. 20:12

J

Jesus said, "I am the way."

John 14:6

Draw the path to our world.

43

Keep your tongue from evil.
Psa. 34:13

L

Look unto me and be saved.
Isa. 45:22

What Does This Code Say?

___ ___ ___ ___ ___   ___ ___
10 5 19 21 19   9 19

___ ___ ___   ___ ___ ___ ___ ___ ___
15 21 18   19 1 22 9 15 18

A	B	C	D	E	F	G	H	I	J
1	2	3	4	5	6	7	8	9	10

K	L	M	N	O	P	Q	R	S
11	12	13	14	15	16	17	18	19

T	U	V	W	X	Y	Z
20	21	22	23	24	25	26

45

My son, give me your heart.
Prov. 23:26

CONNECT THE DOTS

No man can serve two masters.
Matt. 6:24

47

Oh give thanks unto the Lord, for He is good. Psa. 107:1

Draw a face for this girl.

48

Praise the Lord! For it is good to sing praises to our God. Psa. 147:1

CONNECT THE DOTS

49

Quietly wait for the salvation of the Lord. Lam. 3:26

CONNECT THE DOTS

50

R

Remember the sabbath day to keep it holy. Ex. 20:8

CONNECT THE DOTS

51

S

Seek the Lord while He may be found. Isa. 55:6

Help James and John leave their nets to follow Jesus.

Thou God seest me. Gen. 16:13

FINISH THIS DRAWING

53

Unto Thee, O God, do we give thanks. Psa. 75:1

54   Which one is thankful?

Verily, verily, I say to you, whatever you shall ask the Father in my name, He will give it to you. John 16:23

CONNECT THE DOTS 55

ANSWER: NINE

How many animals can you find?

X

Exceeding great and precious promises are given to us. **2 Pet. 1:4**

Here's a Message for You!

HOLY BIBLE

'

_ _ _ _
7   15   4   19

_ _ _ _
23   15   18   4

_ _   _ _ _ _ .
9   19   20   18   21   5

A	B	C	D	E	F	G	H	I	J
1	2	3	4	5	6	7	8	9	10

K	L	M	N	O	P	Q	R	S
11	12	13	14	15	16	17	18	19

T	U	V	W	X	Y	Z
20	21	22	23	24	25	26

Y

You are bought with a price.
2 Cor. 6:20

CONNECT THE DOTS

58

Z

Zion heard and was glad. Psa. 97:8

How many pencils can you find?

ANSWER: 13

We see time passing when winter turns to spring, spring turns to summer, and summer turns to _____. **Genesis 1:14**

60

Joseph had a coat of many _____.

GEN. 37:3

Pharaoh's daughter found baby Moses, in a basket, floating in the Nile River.

EX. 2:5-10

THE TEN COMMANDMENTS*

1. YOU SHALL HAVE NO OTHER GODS BEFORE ME.

2. YOU SHALL NOT MAKE YOURSELVES ANY IDOLS.

3. YOU SHALL NOT USE THE NAME OF THE LORD IN VAIN.

4. REMEMBER THE SABBATH DAY, TO KEEP IT HOLY.

5. HONOR YOUR FATHER AND MOTHER.

6. YOU SHALL NOT KILL.

7. YOU SHALL NOT COMMIT ADULTERY.

8. YOU SHALL NOT STEAL.

9. YOU SHALL NOT TELL LIES.

10. YOU SHALL NOT WANT SOMETHING ANOTHER PERSON HAS.

God gave Moses the ____ _____ as rules to keep.

63

* ABBREVIATED (EXODUS 20:3-17)

David believed that God would help him fight the giant.

I SAM. 17:37

God told Gideon to break down the idols that his people worshipped.

Daniel knew that God was with him in the lions' den.

66

DAN. 6:22

Jonah was swallowed by a great _____ because he ran away from God.

Jesus healed a maniac.

Jesus is knocking at the door.

Connect the Dots.

69

REV. 3:20

CONNECT THE DOTS

Jesus Christ was born in a _____ where the animals ate and slept. Luke 2:1-7

John baptized Jesus in the Jordan River. The Holy Spirit came like a _____ to Jesus. Matthew 3:13-17

Jesus said, "_____ and it shall be opened."

MATT. 7:7

God wants Jimmy to tell his dad about the window he broke. Help him find his dad.

EXODUS 20:16

73

Tom's parents give him chores to do. It is time for Tom to feed the dog. Draw hands on the clock to show six o'clock.   Exodus 20:12

74

When it's time, Sue gets up the first time her mom calls.
She knows God wants her to obey her parents.
Ephesians 6:1

. . . and there is a time to speak.   Ecclesiastes 3:7

There is a time to plant and a time to harvest the crop.
Ecclesiastes 3:2

CONNECT THE DOTS

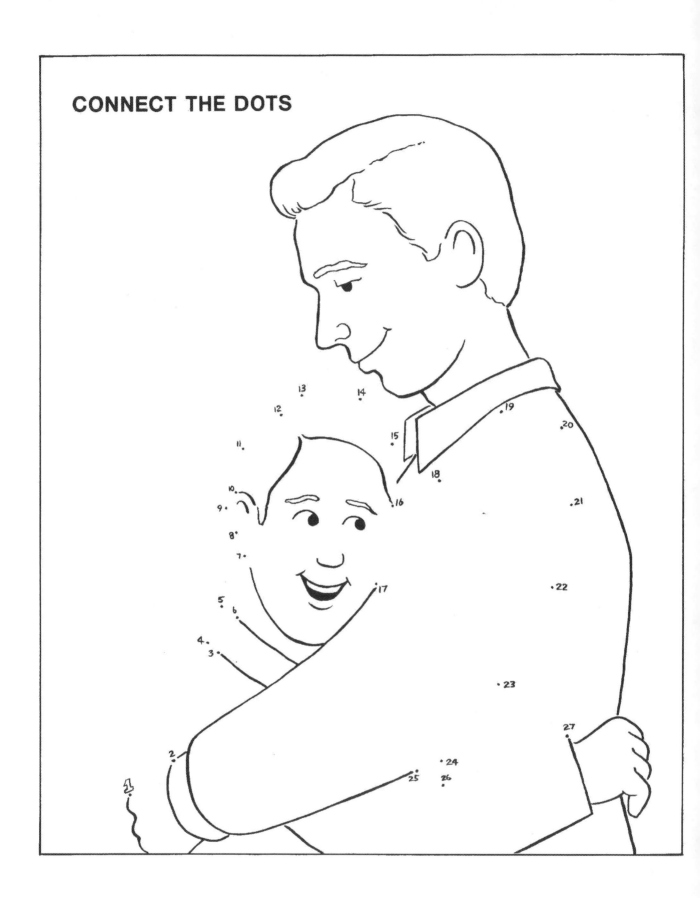

There is a time to love . . .

It doesn't take a lot of time to tell someone "I love you."
1 John 3:23
Can you find eight hearts in this picture?

God Says, "Do Not Steal."

Help this girl and her father visit this sick person.

JAMES 1:27

Jimmy's grandfather is reading a Bible story to him.

JOSHUA 1:8

God wants to shape our lives like a potter
shapes a pot.

ISAIAH 64:8

83

King David said he wanted to know God just as much as a thirsty deer wants to drink water from a cool brook. Help the deer find the water. Psalm 42:1

84

What did Abraham and Isaac find caught in the bushes?

GEN. 22:13

85

Here's a Message for You!

Jesus Said,

"
$\overline{\ \ }$ $\overline{\ \ }$ $\overline{\ \ }$ $\overline{\ \ }$ $\overline{\ \ }$ $\overline{\ \ }$ $\overline{\ \ }$ $\overline{\ \ }$ $\overline{\ \ }$ $\overline{\ \ }$
9   23 9 12 12   14 5 22 5 18

"
$\overline{\ \ }$ $\overline{\ \ }$ $\overline{\ \ }$ $\overline{\ \ }$ $\overline{\ \ }$ $\overline{\ \ }$ $\overline{\ \ }$ $\overline{\ \ }$.
12 5 1 22 5   25 15 21

A	B	C	D	E	F	G	H	I	J
1	2	3	4	5	6	7	8	9	10

K	L	M	N	O	P	Q	R	S
11	12	13	14	15	16	17	18	19

T	U	V	W	X	Y	Z
20	21	22	23	24	25	26

86

— HEB. 13:5

A young woman who believes in Jesus should only marry a young man who believes in Jesus.

These young people are singing for Jesus.

PSA. 81:1

Help this young person follow Jesus to heaven.

PSALM 25:4

Help the prodigal son find his way back to his father.

90

LUKE 15:11-32

A good Samaritan will stop
to _____ a person in need.

LUKE 10:30-37

91

Help this girl take Jesus to her family.

92

JOHN 1:41

God, like a father, protects us from evil if we trust Him.
Draw teeth on the alligator.

Here's a Message

Jesus Says

__ __   __ __ __   __ __ __ __   __ __ ,
9 6   25 15 21   12 15 22 5   13 5

__ __ __ __   __ __ .
15 2 5 25   13 5

A	B	C	D	E	F	G	H	I	J
1	2	3	4	5	6	7	8	9	10

K	L	M	N	O	P	Q	R	S
11	12	13	14	15	16	17	18	19

T	U	V	W	X	Y	Z
20	21	22	23	24	25	26

94
JOHN 14:15

Draw your smiling face here.

95

JOHN 3:16